SWIMWEAR EVOLUTION

Illustrated by Roberto Cruz

Swimwear Evolution – A concise story

Imagine yourself on a beach. The sun is shining, the waves are lapping against the shore, and all is peaceful. Suddenly, a policeman approaches a young woman, and takes her to jail for exposing too much leg. As extreme as this seems, this occurred often in the early 20th century. Until things became the way they are now a great deal of events had to happen. The evolution of swimwear is the story of progressive ladies that dared the status quo of fashion and societal norms, technological advances in textile manufacturing, and war.

Before the 1900s the beach was frequented mostly by people trying to take care of their health, and there was not much need for an adequate piece of clothing to wear in the water. The prevailing style was a burdensome long Victorian bathing suit. By the turn of the century activities such as swimming and diving were becoming more popular and people needed more functional clothing for beach activities.

Swimming suits were redesigned and inspired by sailor uniforms. Not much more practical than their predecessor, they were made from silk or wool and were typically black, knee-length, puffed-sleeve dresses. Women also heavily accessorized with swim caps, umbrellas, long stockings and lace-up bathing slippers.

In 1907, Australian swimming star Annette Kellerman visited the United States. She sported a snugly fitting swimsuit exposing skin on her legs, arms, and neck – similar to a men's swimsuit of the era – and was promptly arrested for it. Despite initial public outcry over Kellerman's supposed indecency, her swimming suit style started to gain popularity. Inspired by it, a company called Jantzen made the first functional bathing suit: a tight one-piece short-sleeved dress used with shorts.

In the 1920s, Jantzen's style swimming suit became very popular. The stockings and shoes were still part of the fashion, and the modern ladies loved using caps and oriental parasols. However modern swimwear started getting smaller and more skin was exposed. This caught the attention of the authorities. Enter the swimwear police. They would walk up and down the beach with a measuring tape in hand making sure women weren't showing more than 6 inches of skin above their knees. The penalty for exposing too much was a heavy fee or even jail time. But the fashion was here to stay, thanks in part to the rise of bathing suit beauty pageants. The first Miss America Pageant debuted in 1921 in Atlantic City, New Jersey. By the end of the decade, the police stopped ticketing for indecency. Despite the lack of controversy, men's swimwear was also evolving: a pair of shorts with a long sleeveless top which exposed more of men's arms and chest. The strong, superman body made a man's torso in vogue at the beach.

In the 1930s, rubber mixed with wool, cotton, rayon or silk threads, called lastex, made bathing suits lighter and more comfortable. These new swimsuits fit more snugly and showed more legs and back than ever before. Modern swimsuits were also available in an increasing range of colors and women could buy them as a one-piece. These smaller swimsuits also encouraged a new beach-going trend made popular by Coco Chanel: suntanning.

Rationing during World War II had a profound effect on the swimsuit industry. Companies were forced to reduce the usage of materials like cotton, wool, nylon, silk and rubber. Savvy entrepreneurs realized they could use less materials and still sell swimsuits and the bikini was born. However, it was considered a bit too revealing for most women which still preferred a one-piece. Most public beaches banned the use of bikinis until the beginning of the '50s.

The 1950s saw more textile innovations and swimsuits becoming fashionable. New brands like Cole of California, Rose Marie Reid, and Elizabeth Stewart started to emerge with swimsuits made of nylon and an improved version of lastex, allowing the suits to dry faster. Colors were bold and patterns like plaid, gingham checks and polka dots were in vogue. Bikinis were no longer banned at the beach and were used by famous actresses in the movies, but the one-piece swimsuits were still preferred by women. Men were now going shirtless on the beach and in athletic competitions. They commonly used swim trunks, which were slightly looser than the swim briefs from the preceding decade. Made with cotton and an elastic waist, they could be found in a wider range of colors, as well as tropical prints.

At the beginning of the 1960s, swimwear was still very conservative, but things changed over the next couple decades. Surf culture became popular and the song 'Itsy Bitsy Teenie Weenie Yellow Polka Dot Bikini' by Brian Hyland was a sensation. Movie stars like Marilyn Monroe and Brigitte Bardot helped popularize modern swimwear, and there was a bikini-buying spree. Men's swim shorts were getting bigger. Called swim-walker shorts, they had elastic bands and pleats on the side to offer more leg room. With the arrival of the hippies in the 1970s came psychedelic colors and a sleuth of new patterns. Spandex, invented in 1958, was now widely used in swimsuit creation improving elasticity and durability and reducing water drag.

In the 1980s, the workout look became popular. Men were obsessed with physical fitness and body building gave popularity to Speedo-style swimsuits. Bathing suits were shiny, colorful, neon and sometimes had animal print. Women wore one or two-piece bathing suits that had a high-cut, V-hip shape and scoop necks. By the late '90s another trend emerged in women's swimwear: the tankini. The two-piece bathing suit consisting of a tank top and a bikini bottom, gave women more modest coverage, since not all of them felt comfortable wearing bikinis or one-piece suits. Men's swimsuits were changing, too. With the advent of professional surfers, modern surf boards became smaller and lighter and surfers needed swimwear that allowed more flexibility of movement on the waves. Calvin Klein subsequently popularized a loosely-fitting surf board short.

In modern times, there has not been much of a change in swimwear fashion in regards of a unique style for our time. What we have instead is a come-back of older fashions giving people more options to choose from: retro, vintage, modern, low-cut, high-waste, nearly every style from the last century.

There is so much choice today, but almost 100 years after the swimwear police first patrolled the beaches, our society is still judging women's swimming suit choices. It was only in 1997, 51 years after the bikini's debut, and 76 years after the Miss America Pageant was founded, that contestants were finally allowed wear a two-piece swimsuit. In 2013, four women were arrested in Myrtle Beach, South Carolina for indecent exposure over Memorial Day weekend. They were wearing thong bikinis – which expose most of the buttocks – and refused to cover themselves after being warned by local authorities. Although not popular in North America, in sunny, exotic Brazil many women choose to use thongs.

No matter the time we are living in or the location, women should have the right to wear whatever style suits them the best. We hope you enjoyed learning more about the history of swimwear and that it inspired you to express your creative self freely - with no judgements.

References:

https://vintagedancer.com
https://en.wikipedia.org/wiki/History_of_swimwear
https://en.wikipedia.org/wiki/History_of_the_bikini
http://dustfactoryvintage.com
https://vintagefashionguild.org/fashion-history/swim-wear-history/
https://floriditaswimwear.com/notable-swimwear-trends-throughout-history/
https://en.wikipedia.org/wiki/Thong_(clothing)
http://www.nydailynews.com/news/national/woman-arrested-wearing-thong-myrtle-beach-article-1.1355434

COLOR TEST PAGE

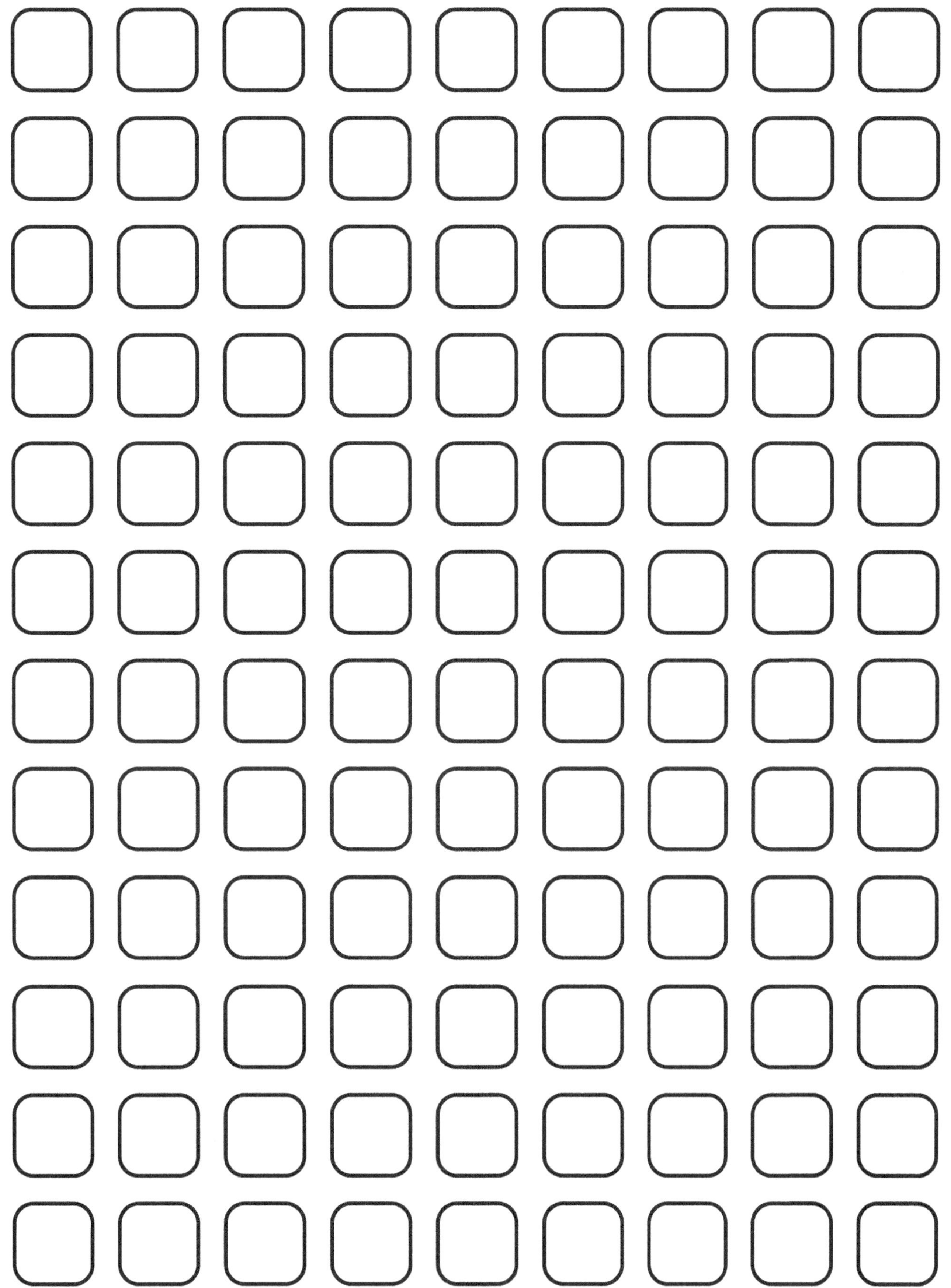

COLOR TEST PAGE

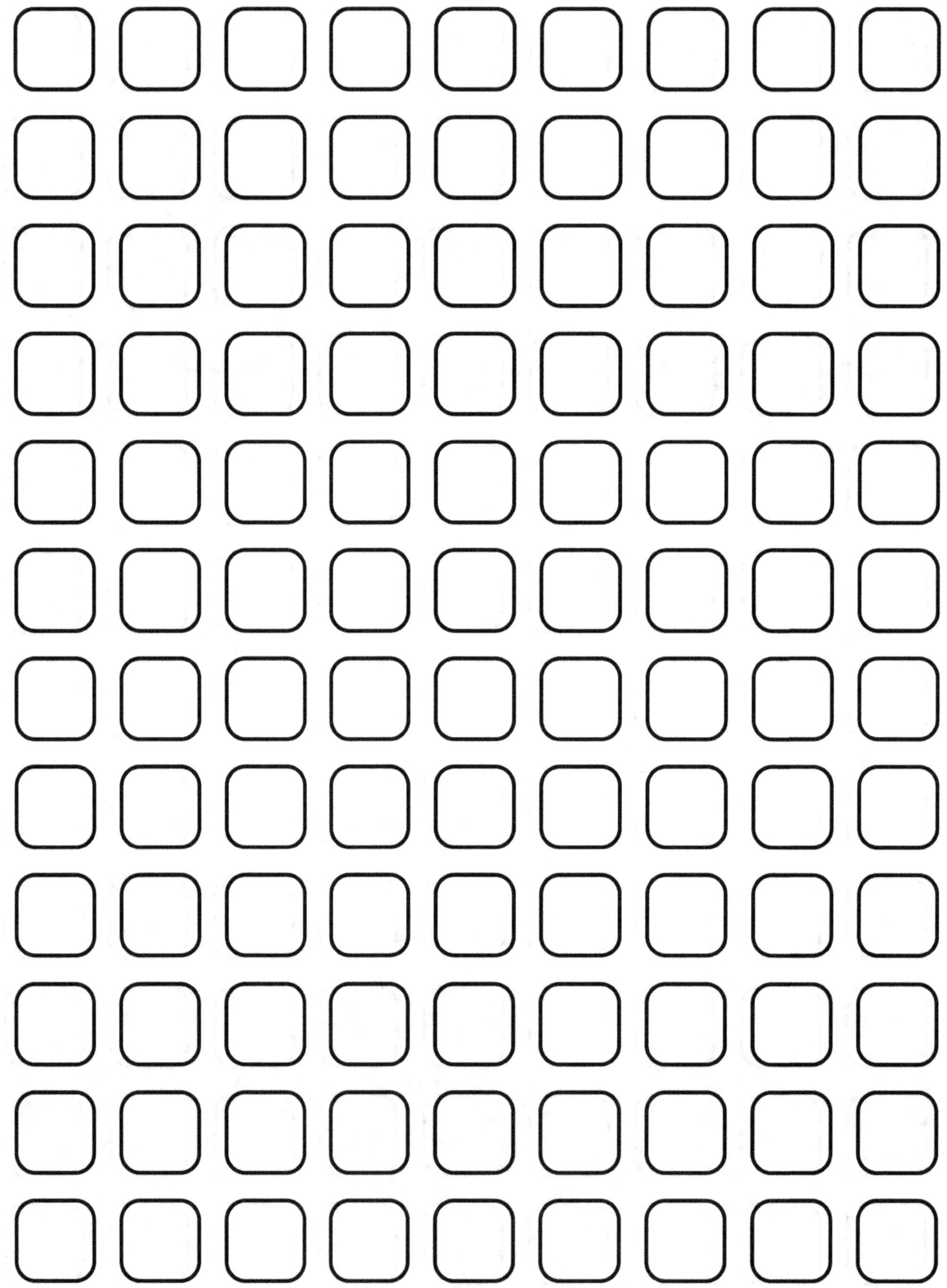

1900s

1900s

1910s

1920s

1920s

Rose
1920s

1920s

1921

1930s

1930s

1940s

1950s

1950s

1960s

1960s

1970s

1980s

1990s

2000s

2010s

LOVE FREE STUFF?

We do, too! Here are a few bonus
images from other *Parachute
Coloring Books* for you to enjoy.

You can find all of our books for sale on Amazon.

Fibonacci: Discovering the Golden Sequence
Behind Nature
A Coloring Book for Adults

The Colors of Fall
Coloring Book

Mother & Daughter
A Narrative Coloring Book

AVAILABLE OCTOBER
Mother & Son
A Narrative Coloring Book

Dear Coloring Book Enthusiast,

Thank you for purchasing our book. We hope you
enjoyed coloring it!
If you have any suggestions or complaints, please reach out
to us on our Facebook page. We are a small independent
business and we strive to make our customers happy. Your
opinion matters to us!

Also, make sure you follow us for free coloring pages, and a
sneak peek of our latest books at:

@parachutecoloringbooks

/parachutecoloringbooks

And if you loved this coloring book:
- LEAVE US A REVIEW ON AMAZON -
This way you will help us to reach other coloring enthusiasts
like you!